Table of Contents

Welcome! **5**

Getting Started **7**

Equipment: Everything You Need **13**

Start Cooking! **27**

Searing Guide **47**

Basic Recipes to Master **56**

  BEEF
    New York Strip 58
    Filet mignon 60
    Flank Steak 62
    Tri-Tip 64
    Corned Beef 66

  PORK
    Pork tenderloin 70
    Pork Chop 72

  CHICKEN
    Chicken Breast 76
    Bone-in Chicken Thighs 78

  LAMB
    Rack of Lamb 82

  SEAFOOD
    Salmon with Hollandaise Sauce 86
    Lobster 88

  EGGS
    Soft Boiled, Poached, Hard Boiled 92
    Egg Bites 93
    Eggs Benedict 95

  VEGETABLES
    Asparagus 98
    Honey Glazed Carrots 99

  DESSERTS
    Crème Brulee 102
    Cheese Cake 104
    Bananas Foster 106
    Wine Poached Pear 108

© 2017 Derek Gaughan. All rights reserved.

For all the latest Sous Vide recipes, reviews, and news, be sure to check out the author's website, [Sous Vide Guy](http://SousVideGuy.com) (http://SousVideGuy.com), home of the most passionate sous vide community!

Warning: Consuming raw or undercooked meats, poultry, seafood, shellfish, eggs or unpasteurized milk may increase your risk of foodborne illness.

WELCOME!

Thanks for checking out Simply Sous Vide! My name is Derek, and ever since I found out about sous vide I've been obsessed with finding new and unique recipes and chasing the Holy Grail that is perfectly cooked meat only achievable through sous vide.

I don't want to waste too much of your time with this obligatory "about me" section, so let's play a quick game of 20 questions.

1. **What's your cooking experience?** I'm just a regular guy who can't cook.

2. **Hold up - why did you write a cookbook if you can't cook?** Great question! The reason why I became obsessed with sous vide is due to its ease of use, predictable results, and most importantly, incredible tasting food. The fact that people who "can't cook" can create jaw-dropping meals with such ease is what pulled me into the sous vide lifestyle. Fast forward a few years and I now run one of the largest sous vide websites, have used every sous vide machine on the market, developed in-depth guides to cooking sous vide, and created delicious recipes – all of which I'm eager to share.

3. **What sous vide machine do you use the most?** I use [Insert Paid Advertising Spot Here]. Hah, just kidding! Honestly, I use quite a few different models interchangeably. Having used all the latest and greatest sous vide machines, I'll share my experience in the equipment section.

4. **What is your favorite thing to cook sous vide?** If we're talking meat (and when aren't we?!), tri-tip steaks are my favorite. A traditionally tougher cut is turned into an amazingly tender steak while also being relatively cheap per pound. I also love making crème brulee, egg bites, and pork tenderloin. Also, everything else.

5. **Why does this game of 20 questions end at 5 questions?** Because you picked out this book to learn how to cook amazing sous vide meals, not who my favorite Pokemon is (Snorlax though - he'd appreciate sous vide to the fullest).

GETTING STARTED

■ Quick History Lesson

You may have heard of sous vide before (pronounced "soo-veed"), but quickly brushed it aside thinking it's something only fancy, elite French chefs can comprehend. While sous vide is a French phrase that translates to "under vacuum", the cooking method is not particularly fancy and it is pretty easy to understand.

Sous vide has a rather rich history dating back to the late 1700s when Sir Benjamin Thompson, a physicist and inventor who focused on thermodynamics, first described the sous vide cooking method in an essay. For those curious, his first sous vide meal was a mutton shoulder.

It wasn't until the 1960s that engineers resurfaced the theory and began adopting sous vide into Michelin-Star restaurants. Fast forward to today and extensive research has gone into understanding the cooking method including proper safety and pasteurization times. What was once exclusive to high-end restaurants is now introduced to the home cook at increasingly lower prices.

■ How it Works

There are two main types of sous vide cooking appliances – all-in-one sous vide machines and immersion circulators (we'll dive into each type shortly). Both types of machines achieve the same outcome, which is cooking food at a consistent and precise temperature.

This is accomplished by vacuum sealing your uncooked food, then immersing the bag in a container of water which your sous vide machine maintains at your precise temperature for an extended period of time (typically around 1-2 hours for meats). At the end of the cook time, your food will be cooked to the precise temperature throughout.

■ Why Sous Vide?

You do not have to be a seasoned master chef to cook **sous vide** – in fact, the equipment and processes are *incredibly* easy. Cheap cuts of meat become juicy and tender, veggies become succulent while retaining more vitamins, and creamy desserts and perfect eggs become a breeze.

Sous vide is a true "set it and forget it" cooking method, kind of like crock pots, but *better*. The reason sous vide is even easier than crockpots is because you can leave your food cooking longer if you're distracted or busy and not worry about overcooking.

That's right, your food will NOT overcook whether you cook it for one hour or 24 hours; the length of time will simply determine its tenderness. Overcooking with a crock pot, oven, frying pan, grill, or any other traditional cooking method and you'll be left with burnt or inedible food, but not sous vide.

CONSISTENT TEMPERATURES

Let's use an example of cooking a medium steak. When using a traditional method, such as pan searing, incredibly hot temperatures are cooking the steak over short periods of time. This means you get a steak with very overcooked edges and a very pink, lukewarm center.

Not only can this discrepancy in temperature be unappetizing, it can also be dangerous as you haven't killed harmful bacteria living in the meat.

On the other hand, with sous vide, I can set the temperature to 135 degrees F and cook the steak to that exact temperature over a period of 1-2 hours. The end result is a steak exactly 135 degrees F, whether it's the center or exterior of the steak. Now you can drop it on a hot pan for a minute or so to develop a nice crust and you have a fancy-restaurant-quality steak!

And even better - by cooking the meat for such a long time, it's possible to pasteurize it and remove the dangerous bacteria.

MORE TENDER MEAT

Many cuts of meat that are traditionally tougher in nature become very tender after cooking them sous vide over longer periods of time. Between 24 – 48 hours, cheap roasts end up lusciously tender and pork shoulders fall apart for the perfect pulled pork.

BETTER FLAVOR

Since the food is vacuum sealed (or simply bagged) beforehand, none of the juices can escape and evaporate. This means your steak can be cooked with all of the amazing flavors that easily escape using traditional cooking methods.

Even better, once you are done cooking, the "escaped" juices are left over in the bag, allowing you to pour it into a pan and create a delicious sauce, if desired. Whoa…now I'm hungry!

INCREDIBLY EASY!

I've been saying it a lot, because it's true! Cooking sous vide is unbelievably easy. You certainly do not need to be a cook in order to start with sous vide. Someone with zero experience can purchase a sous vide machine and have it up and cooking within minutes by simply adding water, adding your food, and waiting! Sous vide machines may be especially beneficial to the following:

- **Busy Parents -**

    Working parents or stay-at-home parents running busy lives can maintain healthy diets and scrumptious meals by cooking sous vide. Since the vast majority of the sous vide process is "hands free", you can easily watch your kids, get some chores done, or even run errands while the meal cooks.

- **Students -**

    We all remember dorm-room-eating – Hot Pockets and ramen. Students can eliminate this junk food by picking up a sous vide machine! Immersion circulators can fit in a backpack and cook pounds of chicken, beef, or vegetables in one session. Also, unlike certain appliances like toasters and toaster ovens, sous vide machines usually aren't banned from dorm rooms.

- **Meal Planners -**

Sunday meal planning has honestly never been easier. This is a big reason why I got into sous vide cooking. Every Sunday I cook up a week's worth of food in water baths and toss them in containers for the week. Perfectly cooked chicken and salmon are always ready to go!

EQUIPMENT: EVERYTHING YOU NEED

Sous Vide Machines

One of the most difficult parts about starting sous vide is deciding which sous vide machine to buy.

New "tech-focused" companies including ChefSteps, Nomiku, Sansaire, and Anova, among others, developed incredible sous vide machines at low costs. So, how do you pick? After all, each machine effectively does the same thing: precisely heat water to a specific temperature. To help you decide which machine to buy, you should first understand the different types available.

ALL-IN-ONE VS IMMERSION CIRCULATOR

The first thing you will want to decide is if you would prefer an all-in-one sous vide machine or immersion circulator. As the name suggests, all-in-one machines (also called sous vide ovens, or water bath sous vide machines) come with the heating element, water circulator, container, lid, and sometimes food racks – everything you need in order to cook, all in a single unit. Immersion circulators on the other hand are small gadgets that attach to the side of a pot or container which only heats the water. With an immersion circulator, you will need to have a water container suitable for cooking (more on containers shortly).

All-in-One Pros

- Simple set up. Simply add water and food, then set your temperature.

- Silent operation. Most all-in-one machines don't have any moving parts, thus no vibration or noise.

- More efficient. These machines use less energy as they are better insulated, close completely, and lose no water to evaporation.

All-in-One Cons

- Much more expensive. These typically run 3-4x the cost of an immersion circulator.

- Fixed capacity. There's no way to expand the capacity of these units if you wanted to say, cook 10 steaks at once.

Immersion Circulator Pros

- Very cheap and affordable.

- Tend to heat water up faster.

- Gives you flexibility with what size and type of containers to use.

Immersion Circulator Cons

- Noisy. Since these machines have to constantly circulate water, they generate noise and some vibrations. The noise levels are similar to a microwave - not terrible, but noticable.

- Less efficient. Water and heat will be lost, especially without a lid. If you want to use a lid, it typically has to be bought specifically to fit your sous vide machine or you need to make one yourself.

STANDARD FEATURES OF ALL SOUS VIDE MACHINES

Many new sous vide machines have fun and unique features to help set them apart from the rest. While these are great selling points, it's important to remember a few of the key features necessary for sous vide machines in order to make the best buying decision.

Water Capacity: If you decide to go with an all-in-one sous vide machine, which includes the water bath, you will want to know how much water the device can hold as you won't ever be able to expand the capacity.

Heater & Circulator: Every sous vide machine has a heating element to get the water to the proper temperature. In an all-in-one machine, the heating element is along the entire base of the unit and the design of the machine ensures all of the water is the desired temperature without the need of a circulator. Immersion circulators need a bit of help making sure all the water is the same temperature. They clip on to the side of your container and in addition to heating the water, they use small propellers to constantly circulate the water. This ensures all of the water is being heated equally.

Temperature Range: Most sous vide machines can reach 200 degrees F or higher.

Temperature Precision: The majority of sous vide machines available claim to keep temperatures within 0.1 degree F.

Safety: The important safety features include low water warning (shuts off when water is too low to prevent burning the unit) and power outage warning (to let you know if the power went out which may spoil food).

UNIQUE FEATURES

As technology advances, creative and powerful sous vide machines are paving the path to a connected kitchen. Multiple manufacturers sell WiFi enabled immersion circulators that let you control the device from even when you're not home. This is particularly useful if you want to start your sous vide cook as you're about to leave work and come home to a perfectly cooked steak. To take it even further, ChefSteps' Joule immersion circulator is 100% app-controlled – that's right, there is no physical interface. Additional creative features include catalogs of sous vide recipes directly tied into your machine.

Sous vide manufacturers are constantly finding new ways to improve their machines and offer new features, so take a look at what differentiating features a sous vide machine has to see if there's any "must-haves" for your lifestyle.

RECOMMENDATIONS

All things considered, my favorite sous vide brands are ChefSteps, Anova, Sansaire, and Grant Creative Cuisine. I'd suggest you check out my blog at
http://sousvideguy.com where you can find reviews of sous vide machines by all of these manufacturers.

If I had to pick only one sous vide machine to use, then I'd currently choose the ChefSteps Joule. The device is controlled via smartphone app rather than physical buttons on the device, which sounds like it could be terrible, but the app is so responsive and reliable that it's a pleasure to use every time.

Containers

If you're one of the many who prefer using immersion circulators to get your perfect sous vide meal, large containers or pots must be used to hold the water for cooking. Certain types are better than others, so let's take a look at our most preferred methods of cooking with **immersion circulators**, in order.

POLYCARBONATE

Polycarbonate water containers and vessels are without a doubt my preferred and recommended water bath for cooking with sous vide immersion circulators. Polycarbonate resists heat very well and is also very lightweight. In addition, they're very cheap to buy on Amazon or your local retail store. One of the other main features to look for in polycarbonate water baths are lids, which help keep even water temperature and prevent water evaporation.

However, fitting an immersion circulator with a lid results in knives and/or power tools to make a choppy cut through the plastic. That being said, a few manufacturers understood this frustration and created polycarbonate sous vide containers and lids with pre-cut holes for each sous vide device. You can actually pick a lid that corresponds to your sous vide machine, such as Anova, Gourmia, or Sansaire. "LIPAVI" is the most popular manufacturer of these custom polycarbonate lids, you can find their products on Amazon.

SHOULD MY CONTAINER BE BPA-FREE?

One question many people often ask is: **are there any BPA-free sous vide water containers?** BPA is always a concern when handling food in plastic, especially when using high temperatures. Years ago, Rubbermaid sold a polycarbonate container on Amazon and claimed it was BPA-free directly in the listing. A few years later, customers noticed the "BPA-free" sticker was no longer on the box or container. After reaching out, Rubbermaid confirmed the containers are NOT BPA-free. Were they ever free of BPA chemicals? I'm not entirely sure... but no need to panic.

BPA is only an issue if it comes in contact with the food you are cooking. With sous vide, our food is wrapped in a vacuum sealed bag or ziplock bag, preventing any BPA chemicals in the container from touching your food. In summary, as long as you are using BPA-free bags to hold your sous vide food, you are absolutely fine! Get whatever container your heart desires.

PLASTIC COOLERS

Plastic coolers, like the durable Coleman coolers you've probably taken on a road trip or to work, are a commonly owned product that people use to cook sous vide. If you plan on using plastic coolers for sous vide, you need to ensure it is large enough. I recommend that it's at least 8" deep and can contain at least 12 quarts of water. Since these coolers are heavily insulated, heat is held very well, so temperature will rise quickly with little power required from the cooker.

POTS

Everyone owns a pot. However not everyone owns one large enough for sous vide! This was the first water container I used when deciding if sous vide was right for me. The downfall of using pots is that you can't use the lid to hold in heat and prevent water evaporation, which requires more power from the cooker. Pots aren't ideal for sous vide due to the following drawbacks:

- Heavy/cumbersome.

- Circular design means less cooking space available.

- No commercially available lids that are compatible with sous vide machines.

KITCHEN SINK

Huh? Yeah, that's not a typo. While we do not encourage the use of kitchen sinks as water containers for sous vide, there have been a number of adventurous home cooks that used their kitchen sink when in a pinch.

Our final verdict on containers: polycarbonate containers are ideal for sous vide. They're cheap and readily available, but that being said there are numerous different water containers that can get the job done. After all, the container simply has to hold heated water. Full rack of ribs in the bath tub, anyone?

Container Lids

We've mentioned lids quite a bit already, and while they are not necessary, having a lid on your container when using **sous vide immersion circulators** is highly recommended for a few main reasons:

1. Helps keep an even water temperature by holding in the heat.

2. Increases energy efficiency by reducing heat loss.

3. Prevents water from evaporating. This may not be too large of a concern when only cooking 1-2 hours. However, when cooking a large roast, evaporation becomes a factor.

4. Prevents contaminants from getting inside.

5. Prevents curious people (or pets) from getting burned.

Now that we've identified the concerns and reasoning behind using water bath container lids, let's look at our options.

First off, many polycarbonate containers are sold with lids. If you own one of these and do not have the matching lid, check out Amazon as they most likely sell it. Polycarbonate lids are also pretty easy to cut a hole large enough to fit the immersion circulator through it, since they stick out over the top of the container. If you are all out of options and cannot get your hands on the lid to your container, or you are using a MacGyver container such as your kitchen sink or beer cooler, you're not out of luck just yet.

- **Aluminum Foil or Plastic Wrap**: Wrap the top of your container in aluminum foil or plastic wrap to help prevent evaporation and hold in some of the heat.

- **Ping Pong Balls**: Yep, this is a weird one. People have placed ping pong balls on top of the water in their container to cover the entire surface which also subside evaporation and heat loss.

Vacuum Sealers

Vacuum sealers are a staple in the sous vide cooking world. After all, sous vide literally translates to "under vacuum". Let's talk about the different types of vacuum sealers and whether or not they are really necessary for sous vide.

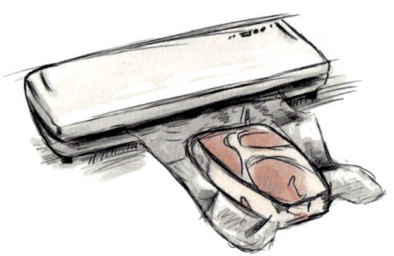

CHAMBER VACUUM SEALERS FOR SOUS VIDE

Chamber vacuum sealers are hands-down the best method for **sealing food for sous vide**, especially if you plan on cooking sous vide frequently. One problem you'll sometimes find with a cheaper vacuum sealer is that liquids can be sucked up from the bag, causing the sealing process to fail and making a mess.

Sous vide chamber vacuum sealers are especially great for sealing bags that contain liquid because the machine doesn't directly suck air from the bag like a vacuum would. To explain it simply, your bag of food is first placed unsealed into the chamber. You then lock the machine shut, which create an air-tight seal. Then, air is removed from both the chamber and your bag of food at the same time, creating a vacuum of no air and no pressure. Since there is no external pressure on the bag, the food/liquid is not agitated and doesn't move. From the outside, it looks like nothing happened! The machine now seals the bag shut, and allows air to rush back into the chamber. When the air comes back in, the bag quickly collapses around your food, giving you a perfect, air--tight seal that never fails.

Another benefit of these chamber sealers is that the costs of bags are much cheaper than your regular FoodSaver type of sealer which uses specifically embossed bags. If you plan on doing a lot of sous vide cooking, chamber vacuum sealers may end up paying for themselves in the long run – though they do cost much more upfront.

EXTERNAL VACUUM SEALER

External vacuum sealers are your typical "edge sealer" that you would find in your local grocery store. The most popular brand, which you've probably heard of, is FoodSaver.

To use an external vacuum sealer, you first place your food and seasonings into a compatible bag. Then, you clamp the vacuum sealer around the open edge of the pack and hit a "Seal" button. The vacuum sealer will first suck out all the air from the bag, making it form-fitting to the food. Finally, the bag uses strips of heating elements to seal the edge of the back shut.

External vacuum sealers will not break the bank like chamber sealers, however the bags are a bit pricier. Nonetheless, these vacuum sealers are usually the best option for those looking to get started with sous vide cooking and are also smaller in size (easier to store in your kitchen). A typical model ranges from $100 – $150 but there are cheaper and more expensive choices out there.

VACUUM SEALER HAND PUMP

If you're really looking to cut down costs, you can give a fully manual hand pump a try. For this system, you get special bags that essentially zip shut, and then you use a small hand pump to suck air from a special air valve on the bag.

There are a few starter kits available for around $20 on Amazon, and one other advantage is the bags are reusable unlike typical vacuum sealed bags.

This system has a few major disadvantages, however -

- Manually pumping air out of bags isn't fun.

- These bags will never get as much air out as the other electric methods, which could lead to uneven cooking temperatures or spoiled food.

- The reusable seal on these bags is not as reliable. If there is a leak, water will get into your food and ruin your meal.

ARE VACUUM SEALERS NECESSARY FOR SOUS VIDE?

Not entirely. It's possible to cook sous vide with regular ziplock bags, but vacuum sealed bags are superior for a number of reason we'll get into shortly.

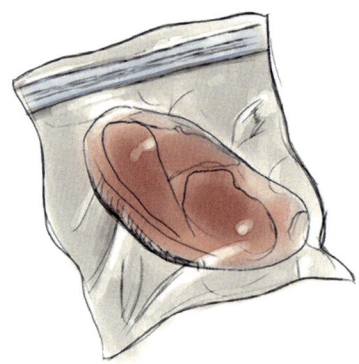

If you want to try ziplock bags for sous vide, you need to purchase the food-grade and freezer-grade type. Once you have your food in the baggie, you can use the **water displacement method** to get a "good enough" seal – this is a fancy physics term for using the surrounding water to eliminate air from the bag.

You leave the zip-lock bag open and slowly submerge the bag into the water. As the bag goes down into the water, the air is pushed out resulting in a decent seal around your food. You then seal the top of the bag and clip it to the side of your container to keep it in place.

Now that I covered an alternative to using vacuum sealers for sous vide, let's talk about the main **benefits of vacuum sealers** and the reasons you should consider investing in one.

WHY YOU SHOULD USE A VACUUM SEALER WITH SOUS VIDE COOKING

Better Surface Heat

Air does not transmit heat as well as water. With a vacuum sealed bag, the bag is tight against the surface of the food which allows the hot water to transfer heat more directly to the food. This results in more consistent cooking temperatures and faster cooking times. The more air pockets you have around your food, the longer it will take for the air to efficiently transmit heat to your food.

Better Flavor

I'm not being scientific here, but it's pretty common sense. Vacuum sealed bags are air-tight and seal in all flavors, juices, and aromas. You can even marinate your food in the vacuum sealed pouch before cooking! And of course, having open baggies (non vacuum-sealed) can result in juices spilling out during cooking, or even worse, having the ziplock baggie sink and next thing you know you're boiling a steak.

Stays Fresh Longer

Outside of sous vide, vacuum sealers play an integral role in keeping food fresh longer, both in the refrigerator and freezer. From a sous vide perspective, vacuum sealing meals in advance for the week not only keeps the food fresh but it's also ready to cook! Simply drop the bag in your water bath and you're good to go. Since the meal is still sealed after cooking, you can even refrigerate the food and place it in an ice bath until you're ready to finish the sear.

Vacuum Sealed Bags Won't Float

Floating bags are not only frustrating, but can even be dangerous. Bags with air float on top of the water which will result in portions of your food not being properly cooked. When cooking sous vide, it's important to always have the food fully submerged in water for even cooking temperatures and safety. Vacuum sealers fully remove any air in your bag prior to your sous vide cook.

Even though the sous vide name specifically references vacuum sealing, they are not 100% necessary for cooking. Nonetheless, we absolutely recommend using a vacuum sealer with cooking sous vide as the benefits largely outweigh the initial cost investment.

Sous Vide Bags

I frequently receive the question, "**what are the best bags for sous vide?**" There are a wide array of sous vide packaging methods available, so the answer to this question largely relies on what you plan on cooking and which benefits are most important to you (cost, reusability, or performance). To help you identify which sous vide bags to use, I ranked them in order of the most preferred methods and also highlighted the major benefits. But first, let's discuss an important and popular topic:

ARE PLASTIC SOUS VIDE BAGS SAFE?

Yes – as long as you buy the right ones. The reason why so many people often question the safety of using plastics with sous vide is because of BPA chemicals and the possibility of melting the plastic or seal. Luckily, nearly all food-grade bags today are BPA-free, and since the bags are BPA-free, you don't have to worry about the plastics in your sous vide container since they won't touch your food. To sum up the question, sous vide plastic bags are perfectly safe if you purchase the correct types – always read the labels before you make a purchase.

Any vacuum sealer bags or bags that are specifically made for sous vide should be fine. If you enjoy using Ziploc bags, just be sure to look for the extra thick "freezer-style" bags which also often say food-grade.

VACUUM SEALER BAGS FOR SOUS VIDE

Vacuum sealer bags are perfectly safe and are the most recommended method for cooking sous vide. Vacuum sealing creates a tight wrap around your food resulting in more surface contact with the hot water and more precise cooking temperatures. In addition, these sous vide bags can be used with high temperatures as the seals resist breaking and spoiling food.

As to which brand or style of bag to use, that's completely up to you. Some vacuum sealer bags are sold in pre-cut sizes, whereas others are sold as continuous rolls.

If you buy a continuous roll of vacuum sealer bags, you unroll your desired length and then seal one end with your vacuum sealer (no need to vacuum since the other end will still be unsealed). While there are some extra steps here in cutting the roll and sealing an edge before you place your food inside, it's cheaper in the long run since it lets you customize every bag to fit your food, which means no wasted plastic or wasted space in your sous vide container.

HEAVY DUTY ZIPLOC BAGS

If you're in a pinch, heavy duty Ziploc bags can be used for sous vide cooks as long as **the cooking temperature is below 158F.** When cooking above this temperature, Ziploc seals can break open resulting in water in your bag and a boiled steak. Some cooks double up on the bags to help prevent this from happening, but again, if cooking at higher temperatures, it's best to just use vacuum sealed bags.

EQUIPMENT: EVERYTHING YOU NEED

ADDITIONAL SUPPLIES FOR SOUS VIDE PACKAGING

CANNING JARS

Canning jars work amazing for multiple sous vide recipes, and best of yet, they're obviously reusable! The most common uses for canning jars with sous vide is pickling and desserts such as crème brule. More recently, Starbucks began selling sous vide egg bites which sparked a sous vide trend of making homemade egg bites in small canning jars.

Canning jars are absolutely safe to use as long as you ensure to not over tighten the lids when cooking because air must be able to escape.

SARAN WRAP

No, you cannot do a full cook with just Saran wrap! However, high quality plastic wrap can be used in conjunction with other methods listed above to help retain the shape of foods. For example, you can wrap your roast in saran wrap to better retain its shape and prevent any herbs in the bag from leaving fossil-like indentations on it.

CLIPS FOR YOUR CONTAINER

If you elect to use ziploc bags or sous vide bags without sealing them, it's highly recommended to clip the bags to the rim of your sous vide container. Doing so prevents spillage or breaking the seal of ziploc bags. It's also much easier to grab your food once the cook is done since you don't have to fish around in hot water.

FOOD RACKS

Food racks are often used while cooking sous vide to help separate food and keep the bags from floating. These stainless steel racks closely resemble dish drying racks and are intended to be placed directly in the water bath. All-in-one sous vide machines often come with a removable food rack; however, if you opt to use an immersion circulator, this optional accessory can be purchased separately.

START COOKING!

Alright, we talked about the equipment and tools used for sous vide cooking. Now how do we actually begin making great food? While the overall process is very straight-forward and easy, there are a few confusing areas that newcomers commonly question. We'll discuss these areas and dive right into our first cook.

■ Quick Overview: Step by Step for Cooking a Steak

PREPARE IT

1. Pre-heat water bath to your ideal temperature (more on this below).

2. (Optional) Season your steak with salt and pepper.

3. Vacuum seal the steak or place it in a heavy duty Ziploc bag using the water displacement method.

COOK IT

1. Place bagged steak in water bath and cook for predetermined time based on the chart below.

2. Remove steak and pat dry with paper towels.

SEAR IT

1. Pre-heat cast iron pan on medium-high heat and add avocado oil (or another high smoke point oil).

2. Sear steak on hot cast iron pan for approximately 1 minute, flipping every 15 seconds.

3. Add butter and any aromatics to the pan for added flavor and crispness. Sear for an additional 30 seconds.

4. (Optional) Break out the searing torch if you're feeling adventurous for a perfect crust.

SERVE IT

1. Before serving, use a spoon to top the steak with the leftover juices and butter from the pan - this will help further develop the crust and add flavor.

2. Cut against the grain. Enjoy!

Preparing Your Food

It's time to pick your food of choice. Typically, people new to sous vide only think of cooking steaks since it's one of the most traditional and iconic cuts of meat for this method of cooking. However, cooking sous vide goes well beyond steaks, and even meat for that matter. A few of my favorite uses for sous vide include perfect eggs (poached, soft boiled, hard boiled, and more) and creative single-serve desserts, such as crème brulee.

Nonetheless, most meats, fishes, and veggies are prepared the same way: season, bag, and seal. The wildcard in that sequence is the seasoning, as it can widely vary depending on the dish. General rule of thumb is to generously salt and pepper your food before sealing it in the bag. You may see recipes for various meats calling to add olive oil or butter to your bag before cooking as well. I disagree with this trend as the fats in butter and oil can actually draw flavors out of your meat instead of adding flavor. Skip the butter. Skip the oil. Stick with salt, pepper, and other spices.

Now that our steak is generously seasoned, simply toss it in a sealable sous vide bag and vacuum seal it (or alternatively, into a Ziplock freezer bag and use the water displacement method). You are now ready to fire up your sous vide machine!

But wait, now that I sealed my food, do I have to begin cooking immediately?

Not at all – toss the sealed food in your refrigerator or freezer until you're ready to cook it. The vacuum sealer will actually help prolong its storage life.

Operating Your Device

Operating your sous vide machine will obviously depend on the model you own, however they are all incredibly easy to use and generally work the same way. I'll break this down depending on the type of machine you own.

ALL-IN-ONE SOUS VIDE MACHINE

It can't get any easier than this! You have everything you need in order to cook sous vide. Simply fill your machines' water bath according to the manufacturer's recommendations – typically there's a minimum and maximum level. Having too little of water can break the device, so be sure to never operate it without water in it.

Once the water is added, simply place your bagged food into the water bath. Many all-in-one machines come with food racks to help hold your food in place so it doesn't float. Once all your food is added, close the lid, plug the device in, and set your temperature (more on this in the next section).

IMMERSION CIRCULATORS

Like I mentioned earlier, immersion circulators need a separate water bath. Fill your container with enough water to fully submerge your food, but also ensuring it's within your devices' minimum/maximum water levels. Attach the circulator to your container with the included clip/clamp and plug the device in. After powering on, you can set your preferred temperature based on the guides below.

Temperature/Time Reference Tables

The following temperature and time graphics are courtesy of Grant Creative Cuisine, makers of a variety of sous vide products.

BEEF

There's much to learn about cooking beef sous vide, but don't let that intimidate you. The complexity arises from whether a cut is tender or tough, thick or thin. As a rule of thumb, thinner and tender cuts require less cooking time than thicker and tougher ones.

The sous vide time and temperatures for all these permutations are covered in our handy beef temperature chart below.

To start, try the tender and/or thinner cuts and slowly progress to the larger roasts as you familiarize yourself with how time and temperature affects meat texture. For larger, tougher cuts that require longer cooking times, make sure you sear the surface of the meat beforehand and follow the recommended time and temperature settings.

DID YOU KNOW?

- The hide from one cow can make 20 footballs.

- Uruguay, New Zealand, Argentina, Australia and Brazil are the only countries with more cows than people.

- Cows can hear lower and higher frequencies better than humans.

- Cows are pregnant for 9 months just like people.

Cooking Beef Sous Vide
A quick and easy guide

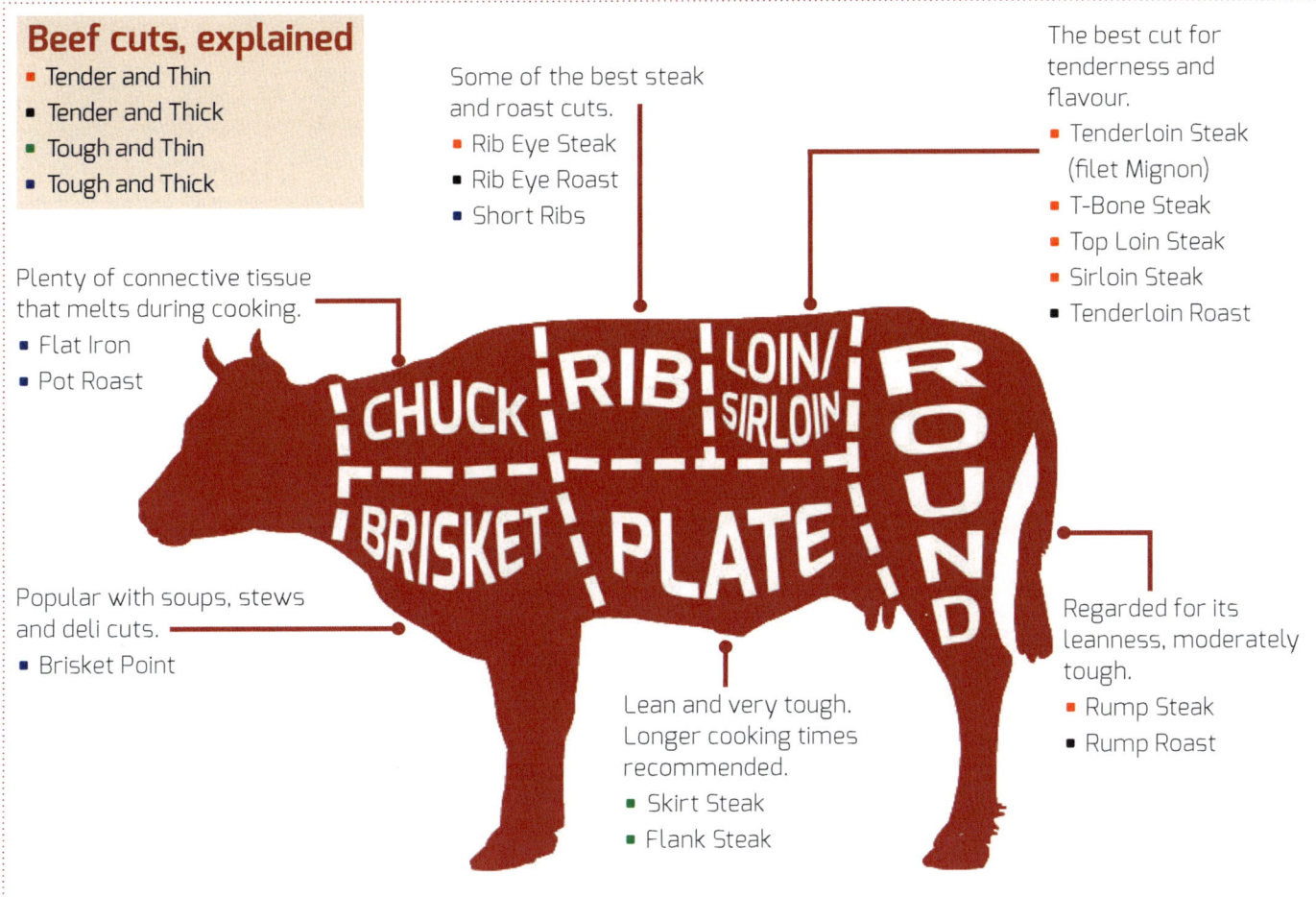

Beef cuts, explained
- Tender and Thin
- Tender and Thick
- Tough and Thin
- Tough and Thick

Some of the best steak and roast cuts.
- Rib Eye Steak
- Rib Eye Roast
- Short Ribs

The best cut for tenderness and flavour.
- Tenderloin Steak (filet Mignon)
- T-Bone Steak
- Top Loin Steak
- Sirloin Steak
- Tenderloin Roast

Plenty of connective tissue that melts during cooking.
- Flat Iron
- Pot Roast

Popular with soups, stews and deli cuts.
- Brisket Point

Lean and very tough. Longer cooking times recommended.
- Skirt Steak
- Flank Steak

Regarded for its leanness, moderately tough.
- Rump Steak
- Rump Roast

Beef temperature chart

			Tender		Tough	
	Temperature	Timing	Thin 1.0 - 1.5 inches	Thick 2 - 3 inches	Thin 1 - 1.5 inches	Thick 2 - 3 inches
			Time to pasteurize			
Rare	50°C 122°F		Not Recommended			
Medium Rare	55°C 131°F	1 - 2 hours	2.5 - 3 hours	4.5 - 6.5 hours	24 hours	36 - 72 hours
Medium	60°C 140°F		1.5 - 2 hours	2.5 - 4 hours		
Done	70°C 158°F		1 - 1.5 hours	2 - 3 hours		

www.grantcreativecuisine.com
enquiries@grantcreativecuisine.com

LAMB

When buying lamb, just like beef, choose the leaner cuts since you don't need the fat for it to taste amazing. Lamb's intense, rich and earthy flavor works not just with the usual mint sauce, but stronger aromatics like cumin and paprika too.

In this guide, we'll explore 4 cuts in particular:

Steak, rack, neck fillet, and shanks. These serve as a solid introduction to cooking lamb sous vide. Neck fillet and shanks are definitely my favorites - they are super tender and unbelievably juicy after the low and slow treatment!

DID YOU KNOW?

- In 1996, a sheep named Dolly was the first mammal to be cloned from a somatic cell.

- China has the largest number of sheep in the world.

- Like various other species including humans, sheep make different vocalizations to communicate different emotions. They also display and recognize emotion by facial expressions.

Cooking Lamb Sous Vide
A quick and easy guide

Lamb cuts, explained
- Thin
- Thick
- Extra Thick

One of the tougher cuts, generally sold for stews or grinding. It also is perfect for low and slow cooking!
- Neck Chop
- Neck Fillet Roast

The 'jewel of the lamb', very tender and flavourful.
- Sirloin Chop
- Loin Roast
- Loin Chop

Often sold as two separate joints, blade and arm (knuckle). As well as cooked whole, shoulder can also be trimmed, cubed and cooked in casseroles or curries.
- Arm Chop
- Blade Chop
- Shoulder Roast

Flavoursome and nutritious, a prime cut with very little fat. A lamb shank is the bottom cut of the leg.
- Chump
- Shank
- Leg of Lamb

The rack of lamb is a tender, flavoursome and highly prized cut. The breast is cheaper but highly versatile.
- Skirt Steak
- Flank Steak

Lamb temperature chart

			Tender	Tough	
	Temperature	Timing	Thin 1 - 1.5 inches	Thick 1.5 - 2.5 inches	Extra Thick 3 inches
			Time to pasteurize		
Medium Rare	55°C 131°F	1 hour	2.5 - 3.5 hours	8 - 24 hours	24 - 48 hours
Medium	60°C 140°F		1.5 - 2 hours		
Done	70°C 158°F		1 - 1.5 hours		

www.grantcreativecuisine.com
enquiries@grantcreativecuisine.com

POULTRY

Chicken, turkey and duck are amazing when cooked sous vide. Poultry is super juicy when cooked sous vide and there's endless possibilities for seasonings and recipes.

All you need to know when it comes to sous vide poultry is the differences in optimal temperatures for white versus dark meat. With the exception of duck, chicken and turkey breast meat are considered white whereas the rest (wings, thighs, drumsticks) are dark meat.

In general, dark meat has higher optimal temperatures than white meat. Due to these differences, it's best to break down the parts (i.e. not cook a whole bird in one piece) for sous vide cooking. Please refer to the Poultry temperature chart below for guidance.

We recommend going boneless for breast as it's easier to serve right away, or portioned into slices.

For duck breast, the optimal temperature ranges from 57°C (135°F) for medium rare to 70°C (158°F) for well done depending on your preference. The temperature charts on the next page reflect our recommended "doneness".

A final tip on getting duck skin crispy (especially for breasts) as the skin is quite thick is to pan fry it over a medium heat for 5-6 minutes until golden. Be careful with adding sweet sauces or marinades to the skin as it'll caramelize and burn the skin before it gets nice and crispy.

DID YOU KNOW?

- **The chicken is the closest living relative of the T-Rex, and there are more chickens on the planet than people.**

- **It's possible for a chicken to live without its head. Mike the headless chicken lived for 18 months without a head in 1945, went on tour, and was even featured in Time and Life magazine.**

Cooking Poultry Sous Vide
A quick and easy guide

The wing has 3 segments: the drummette, the middle 'flat' segment containing 2 bones and the tip. Wings are often served as a light meal or bar food, including the Buffalo Wing, invented in 1964. Wings are generally not cooked sous vide - try barbecuing.

The breast is the leanest cut and high in protein. Chicken and turkey are considered white meat, but duck breast is dark. Traditional cooking methods yield relatively tough results, but this is where sous vide shines!

The leg is darker and fattier than the breast meat. Comprised of the drumstick (lower part) and the thigh (upper part). Duck and turkey legs perform best under longer cooking times - good things come to those who wait!

Poultry temperature chart

	Thickness	Temperature	Timing	Time to Pasteurize
Chicken Breast	1 - 1.5 inches	62°C 149°F	1 - 3 hours	2 hours
Chicken Leg		65°C 140°F	1.5 - 3 hours	2.5 hours
Duck Breast		58°C 136.5°F	1 - 3 hours	2 hours
Duck Leg	1 - 2 inches	70°C 158°F	8 - 12 hours	
Turkey Breast	1.5 - 2 inches	62°C 143.5°F	1.5 - 3 hours	2.5 hours
Turkey Leg	1 - 2 inches	70°C 158°F	8 - 12 hours	2 hours

www.grantcreativecuisine.com
enquiries@grantcreativecuisine.com

PORK

Although not necessary for pork, brining improves moisture retention and can enhance bite and texture for leaner cuts of pork such as tenderloin (filet) and chops.

Pork shoulder is a leaner, tougher cut that benefits from longer and slower cooking. Pulled pork is just one way to showcase how tender and juicy it can be, with not many fancy additions needed. Pork is a great ingredient and cooked sous vide is perfect for feeding a crowd.

DID YOU KNOW?

- Pork tenderloin cuts are almost as lean as skinless chicken breast.

- Weight-wise, pork is by far the most widely consumed meat, with about 100 tons eaten annually.

- There are about a billion pigs in the world at any one time.

Cooking Pork Sous Vide
A quick and easy guide

Pork cuts, explained
- Thin Cuts 1.0 - 1.5 inches
- Thick Cuts Up to 2.5 inches

The back section along both sides of the backbone. Includes the tenderloin, the leanest and most tender cut. Also provides the back ribs.
- Tenderloin/Fillet
- Chops and Steak
- Boneless Roasts or Joints
- Baby Back Ribs

A very versatile cut. The pork shoulder provides the highest level of marbling, perfect for roasting or braising.
- Shoulder Joint
- Shoulder Steak

A tougher cut, cooking low and slow makes the meat more tender.
- Tenderloin Roast
- Leg Joints

Belly pork is wonderfully rich - and value for money! Cooking low and slow reduces the fat and results in luscious and succulent indulgence.
- Spare Ribs
- Belly Joint

Pork temperature chart

	Temperature	Timing	Thin	Thick
			Time to pasteurize	
Pink & Moist	56 - 58°C 133 - 136°F	1.5 - 2 hours	2.5 hours	Not recommended
Traditional Style	60°C 140°F		2.5 hours	
Soft & Moist	60 - 65°C 140 - 149°F	24 - 48 hours	Not recommended	4 hours
Traditional Style	75°C 167°F	8 - 12 hours		2.5 hours

www.grantcreativecuisine.com
enquiries@grantcreativecuisine.com

SEAFOOD

Delicate ingredients such as fish and shellfish are prone to overcooking, rendering them rubbery and too firm. The gentle sous vide treatment brings out the best in them so do make sure you get fresh and high quality seafood. You'll get to try amazing new textures too, such as a lightly cooked, buttery medium-rare salmon that is slightly flaky yet very tender.

Seafood is an easy ingredient to master with sous vide as it cooks quicker and has less time and temperature variation overall. This gives you the opportunity to be more creative about food plating and presentation.

DID YOU KNOW?

- **The mantis shrimp has claws with an incredibly fast and powerful strike, launching with the velocity of a bullet, capable of breaking aquarium glass.**

- **The pistol shrimp can deliver an explosive attack hotter than the surface of the sun and loud enough to rupture a human ear drum.**

Cooking Seafood Sous Vide
A quick and easy guide

Lobster, Shrimp & Scallops
Shelled, 52°C (125.5°F) and a cooking time of 20 - 30 minutes maximum.

Lean Fish
Examples are cod, haddock, plaice, hake, lemon sole, monkfish, pollock, mullet, red snapper, sea bass, sea bream and turbot. Great results when cooked medium rare at a temperature of between 47°C - 50°C (116.5°F - 122°F) for 20 - 30 minutes depending on thickness.

Oily Fish
Examples are tuna, trout, swordfish and salmon. They can be enjoyed rare at 43°C (109.5°F) for a different experience, or more commonly medium rare at 47°C - 50°C (116.5°F - 122°F). For those who prefer it more 'done', go for medium at 55°C - 60°C (131°F - 140°F). Again, cook for 20 - 30 minutes, depending on thickness.

Note: For salmon, an extra brining step is necessary before cooking sous vide. This prevents the secretion of white protein (albumin) when cooked, firms up the fish for easier handling and preserves the vibrant orange colour even when it's cooked.

Seafood temperature chart

	Temperature	Thickness	Time
Rare	43°C / 109°F	0.5 inches	20 mins
Medium Rare	50°C / 122°F	1 inch	30 mins
Medium	60°C / 140°F		

Note: The times below are not pasteurized times and therefore should not be served to immuno-compromised individuals.

To pasteurize fish and shellfish (up to 1 inch thick), the quickest way is to cook them medium at 60°C (140°F) for 1.5 hours.

www.grantcreativecuisine.com
enquiries@grantcreativecuisine.com

EGGS

Eggs are the perfect ingredient to start with in sous vide cooking and are a favorite within the sous vide community. The results are fun, easy, and impressive, plus you don't even need a bag to cook them in! Just gently place them in the sous vide water bath with a spoon and cook at the target temperature for a set amount of time. Once done, serve them straight from the shell onto the plate.

Eggs are very temperature sensitive. Their texture can change drastically within the 60°C - 65°C (140°F - 149°F) range. Egg white starts coagulating at 60°C (140°F) and completely sets around 80°C (176°F); whereas egg yolk starts coagulating at 65°C (149°F) and sets at 70°C (158°F).

With that knowledge, you can construct your perfect egg by choosing the consistency of yolk and white that you like - check out the egg temperature chart below. The 63°C (145.5°F) egg is a popular favorite for a poached egg substitute, because you'll get a custardy yolk that is so good and creamy that you'll want to mop it up with everything on your plate.

DID YOU KNOW?

- White hens produce white eggs, brown/red hens produce brown eggs.

- You can have eggs within eggs, and even multiple-yolked eggs. The largest number of yolks recorded in an egg was 9.

Cooking Eggs Sous Vide
A quick and easy guide

Sauces - Flowing Cream
Fully cooked to delicate runniness. Perfect for egg-based sauces, spaghetti carbonara or the exotic Asian 'half-boiled egg'.

Soft Boiled Eggs - Viscous Honey
The perfect soft-boiled egg. Custardy whites and a thick, honey-like yolk. Never settle for less at breakfast!

Poached Eggs - Thick Mayonnaise
The egg white and yolk are at the same luscious consistency, creating a perfectly poached egg that smoothly slides out of its shell.

Hard Boiled Eggs - Pliable Camembert
The yolk forms a rich, golden truffle. Firming the whites (see below) creates a tender, melt-in-your-mouth hard-boiled egg.

Egg temperature chart

	Flowing Cream	Viscous Honey	Thick Mayonnaise	Pliable Camembert
Temperature	61.5°C / 143°F	63°C / 145.5°F	64°C / 148°F	68°C / 154.5°F
Timing	60 mins			

Optional: Firming the Whites
After sous vide cooking, egg whites are lightly set at a custardy texture. To bring the whites to a firm, peelable solid form without affecting the yolks:

Step 1: Cool
Your eggs - running tap water is perfect.

Step 2: Boil
Your eggs at 100°C (212°F) for 4 minutes.

Step 3: Cool
Your eggs again to yummy perfection.

www.grantcreativecuisine.com
enquiries@grantcreativecuisine.com

VEGETABLES

84°C (183°F) is your magic number for most vegetables and legumes. This is because they contain pectin - the molecular 'glue' that holds the cells together - that only starts to break down at 84°C (183°F). Sous vide cooked vegetables and legumes are tender yet retain their bite (no more mushiness), with a stronger, sweeter, and more concentrated natural flavor as it cooks in its own juice.

Two things to note though: do take extra care when dealing with higher temperatures for vegetables - they'll scald this time, unlike the usual 55°C (131°F) range! Also, here's where having a chamber vacuum sealer may help in achieving a proper seal (since certain odd shapes of vegetables may make it trickier to remove air) as well as trying out new techniques such as compression and quick-pickling.

DID YOU KNOW?

- Eating garlic can keep mosquitoes away - not just vampires!

- Red and yellow bell peppers have four times as much vitamin C as oranges.

- The tomato is botanically a fruit, but was declared a vegetable by the US Supreme Court in 1893.

Cooking Vegetables Sous Vide
A quick and easy guide

Root Vegetables
Beet, carrot, potato, turnip, yam, daikon (Japanese radish), parsnip, celeriac, sweet potato, water chestnut, artichoke.

Note: Up to 1 inch thick. Chop, dice or split them as needed.

Legumes
Beans (borlotti, navy, black, utter, azuki, pinto etc), Chick peas, lentils.

Note: Pre-soak beans for 6-8 hours beforehand. Cook with sufficient liquid (water or stock) in the bag as the beans will absorb them. Don't forget to add your flavouring (herbs, oil, salt etc).

Other Vegetables
Corn, eggplant (aubergine), fennel, onion, butternut squash.

Note: Up to 1 inch thick. Chop, dice or split them as needed.

Vegetable temperature chart

	Types	Temperature	Thickness	Time
Vegetables	Root Vegetables	84°C 183°F	Up to 1 inch	1 - 4 hours
	Other Vegetables	84°C 183°F	Up to 1 inch	45 mins - 2 hours
	Legumes — Beans	84°C 183°F	Not Recommended	6 - 24 hours
	Legumes — Chick Peas			6 - 9 hours
	Legumes — Lentils			1 - 3 hours

www.grantcreativecuisine.com
enquiries@grantcreativecuisine.com

FRUIT

84°C (183°F) is ALSO your magic number for most fruits as they contain pectin similar to veggies.

However when creating your own fruit cocktails and dessert dishes, it is sometimes favorable to cook fruits at low temperatures as it prevents the cells from completely breaking down and to help the fruit keep its form whilst giving you the same superb flavor you get from the low and slow treatment.

Cooking fruits sous vide at a lower temperature also ensures they retain their bite (no more mushiness), with a stronger, sweeter, and more concentrated natural flavor as it cooks in its own juice.

All fruit can be cooked sous vide but the cooking time and temperature need to be adjusted depending on the firmness of the fruit. It is also worth taking into consideration the fruits ripeness as this will also cause your cooking times to vary.

DID YOU KNOW?

- A strawberry isn't an actual berry, but a banana is.

- Apples, peaches, and raspberries are all members of the rose family.

- The color orange is named after the orange fruit, but before that, it was called Geoluread (yellow-red).

- Humans share 50% of their DNA with bananas.

Cooking Fruit Sous Vide
A quick and easy guide

Everyday Fruit
Melon, apple, pear, mango, blueberry, strawberry, blackcurrant, cranberry, grapes, kiwi.

Note: Amazing cooked with flavoured syrups, juice, tea, vinegar etc.

Traditional & Seasonal Fruits
Rhubarb (tender stem), peach, nectarine, plum, apricot, damson.

Note: Great with flavoured syrups (vanilla especially).

Exotic Fruits
Pineapple, pomegranate, passion fruit.

Fruit temperature chart

	Types	Temperature	Time
Fruit	Everyday Fruit	58°C - 84°C 136.5°F - 183°F	45 mins - 90 mins
	Traditional & Seasonal Fruits	60°C 140°F	30 mins - 1 hour
	Exotic Fruits	80°C 176°F	90 mins

Note: Times & temperatures will vary dependent on the sous vide dishes you are creating. Sous vide cocktails for example tend to be prepared using a lower temperature setting of 58°C (136.5°F).

www.grantcreativecuisine.com
enquiries@grantcreativecuisine.com

SEARING GUIDE

Whether you're cooking a steak, chicken breast, or a full rack of ribs, obtaining a crispy sear is crucial. Traditionally, these cuts of meat were cooked on a pan, in an oven, or on a grill, so that sought-after crisp outside was obtained every time.

Sous vide, however, leaves your perfectly cooked meat without a crisp crust. Because of this, properly searing your sous vide food is absolutely necessary. Luckily, there are a whole slew of ways we can achieve this, and I'm going to lay out the steps to obtain the perfect sear for sous vide.

TO PRE-SEAR OR NOT TO PRE-SEAR?
Pre-searing is the act of searing the outside the meat before you start your sous vide cook. This can help you get an extra thick crust with less risk of overcooking during your post-sous vide sear.

I personally feel pre-searing is an unnecessary step since it IS possible to get a perfect crust by only searing after your sous vide cook. If you wish to experiment with pre-searing then have at it, but you should always post-sear in addition to get that perfect, crispy outside to your food.

Methods and Equipment for Searing Sous Vide Food

There are plenty of different ways to sear sous vide steaks, roasts, and virtually any cut of meat. Of course, some methods are better than others – so we ranked them in order from best to worst.

PAN SEAR

Pan searing is hands down the best method for searing sous vide food, especially steaks. If your food can fit in a pan, it's usually the best option. Pans can be preheated to extremely high temperatures for that hot-and-fast sear. The downside? The clouds of smoke such a hot pan can generate can often be grounds for divorce and family hardship from constantly setting off all of the smoke alarms. Luckily, my step by step searing guide below will minimize the smoke and help save your marriage!

Cast Iron Pan

Cast iron is a staple of the culinary world and a product every sous-vider should own. Cast iron holds temperatures extremely well – once it's hot, it stays hot for a long time. They will also outlive all of us due to their durability (queue existential crisis) and can be purchased for very cheap, often around 20 bucks. Most of us probably already own one of these, so you're good to go.

Carbon Steel Pan

If you don't already own a cast iron, and want to try something a bit different and equally as good as cast iron, take a look at carbon steel. Carbon steel pans retain heat equally as well but also have a few different characteristics including:

- Sloped walls allow for flipping food. Cast iron are usually vertical.
- A bit lighter in weight.

Stainless Steel

Finally, we have stainless steel. I rarely use this to sear sous vide food, because the above two are better. However, stainless steel is definitely better for acidic foods since cast iron and carbon steel are reactive metals and cannot cook acidic foods for long periods of time without releasing a metallic-taste. If you're searing any sous vide meat, go with cast iron or carbon.

SOUS VIDE SEAR TORCH

Whenever friends or relatives see me break out a torch for cooking they think I'm crazy (and who can argue?). But the torch serves a great purpose for sous vide, and who doesn't want to play with a torch?!

I honestly think every at-home sous vider should own a searing torch when they're ready to take their cooking to the next level, specifically in regards to obtaining the perfect sear.

The best way to use a torch is in addition to pan searing. You can use a torch to sear sous vide food by itself, but that often takes quite a while and can end up changing the flavors of the food after a while. Break out that torch as soon as you lay your steak in a pan of hot oil and start searing the top end of the steak while the bottom is on the pan; flip it over and repeat. The entire process should only take a minute.

PROS	CONS
Won't overcook the center.	Takes long to get a good sear by only using the torch
Can be used in addition to other searing methods or as a standalone method.	Some torches can affect the taste (butane-type-of-flavors), but most searing models do not.

While we're on the topic of sous vide torches, let's take a look at two of the most popular types available on the market.

Sansaire Searing Kit

Sansaire, one of the big players in the sous vide industry and maker of the Sansaire immersion circulator, also sells an impressive sous vide searing kit. The Sansaire searing kit comes with an intense 2,200 degree F searing torch, searing rack, and a drip tray. The flame on this thing is BIG and is amazing at searing roasts and big cuts of meat with odd shapes that are hard to fully sear in pans. The price is up there, but the flame on this thing is bigger than any other kitchen torch I've seen.

Searzall

The Searzall is actually an add-on torch accessory and not an actual torch. Instead of using a thin flame to sear a cut of meat, which could take quite some time, the Searzall uses the same intense heat from the torch flame but speeds up the process by distributing the temperature. Searzall is especially beneficial if you plan on using torch-only to obtain a sear because it has the wider spread heat and also reduces the potential "gas taste" that butane torches can result in.

OVEN

You can obtain a sear with your oven by simply preheating it to, say 300 degrees, or by using your broiler. Often times the broiler is better for a quick sear to smaller cuts while using the actual oven can help obtain a rich bark on larger roasts. Similar to grilling, using your oven to sear sous vide food is mainly beneficial for larger cuts, such as roasts, which may be hard to sear in a pan or too time consuming for a blow torch. We've had great success using our oven to crisp up eye of round roasts, pork shoulders, and ribs.

PROS	CONS
Next best indoor method behind pan searing for larger cuts (roasts)	Less direct surface contact
Incredibly easy	Easier to overcook internal temps

GRILLING

Grills are traditionally great at getting that thick dark crust we know and love; however, this is obtained from long, direct contact to the flames below it. And since the trick to the perfect sous vide sear is hot and fast, gas grilling is not the perfect method. However, we did place this above smoking because charcoal grills CAN get hot enough for a quick sear. Nonetheless, there are good and bad aspects of using a grill for searing sous vide meats, so let's take a look at the pros and cons.

PROS	CONS
Easy to sear larger cuts, such as a rack of ribs	Less direct surface contact
Easier to sear in bulk (ie. cooking for a lot of people)	Potentially bad weather...
Potentially nice weather!	

SMOKING

Smoking can get an amazingly rich crust, and is particularly good on sous vide smoked briskets. Since smoking uses a "low and slow" method, it's important to make sure you either A) immediately place your food into an ice bath after the sous vide cook and before the smoker in order to lower the internal temperature or B) refrigerate it overnight and finish the cook in a smoker the next day. The reason for this is that the smoker will raise the overall temperature of the meat and overcook it, ruining the whole point of sous vide. Long story short, if you plan on using a smoker to develop your sear, make sure to not overcook it!

PROS	CONS
Easy to get a crust on larger cuts	Low and slow heat
You get the delicious smokiness	Requires chilling of meat beforehand to prevent overcooking

DEEP FRY

While technically not a sear, deep frying is another method to attain crispiness for sous vide meats; however, we personally do not use this very often. We much prefer getting a dark crust from the above methods first.

Step by Step Guide for the Perfect Sear

PAN SEAR + TORCH = BEST SEAR

After tons of testing, I've concluded that the combination of pan searing and torching results in the best sear. When many people purchase their torches, they rely way too much on it and some even skip the pan entirely. I DO NOT recommend using a torch only. This gives an off-flavored combination of burnt steak and maybe even gas (depending on your torch model). Torches do not get a deep enough of a crust to be a proper sear for steaks. However, they are perfect for searing the areas of the steak that the pan did not touch and for further developing the crust from the pan. Doing this successfully will result in a mouth-watering appearance and unbelievable outside crisp.

I also mentioned above that my method involves much more than simply getting a good sear – it saves marriages. My wife used to sigh when she saw me break out one of my sous vide machines because she knew that meant smoke alarms going off later on when it come time to sear. My stove vent is not nearly powerful enough to handle the smoke that develops from following most searing guides (which is to get avocado or peanut oil to its smoking point before even starting - WRONG!). So I set out to find a sear that works without filling the house with smoke.

Step 1: Heat Cast Iron Pan on MEDIUM HIGH

What is this guy crazy? How can I sear a steak on medium? Cast iron pans take a bit to really heat up, so add your avocado oil (or another high smoke point oil, such as grape seed oil) to the pan and let it heat up for a few minutes. Use a digital infrared thermometer to check the surface temperature of your pan. Anything about 350 or above will sizzle. I aim for 450 degrees and had my burner between 6 and 7 out of 9. One of the main reasons people smoke their houses out is because they crank the pan on high heat, and then once the smoke starts billowing they turn the heat down. But the issue is, cast iron pans hold heat so well, that turning down your heat will take quite some time to feel the affect. So the key is to not even let that happen.

Step 2: Add Steak, Flip Often

Dry your steak very well by patting it dry with paper towels. You can test the temperature of your pan by putting only a corner of the steak down. If it's not sizzling (or starts smoking too much), adjust the temperature accordingly and wait. If the oil sizzles when placing the steak in the pan, you should be good to go. An even better method to ensure your pan is preheated to the optimal temperature is to grab a cheap digital infrared thermometer - you can find these on Amazon for under $20. Simply point the thermometer in the pan to read the temperature. Anything over 350F will begin to sizzle, however 450F is an ideal searing range. Once you've determined the pan is ready, add your steak and flip often. I flip about every 15 seconds or so making sure to also get the sides and edges. It's all said and done in about 1 minute flat.

Step 3: Add Butter to Pan

I think this step really helps to develop a crust and adds great flavor. After you do the initial sear for about a minute, add butter to the pan and continue searing for an additional minute, flipping in between.

Step 4: Remove Steak and Torch

If you have a torch, place the steak on a drip tray/grill grate and break out the torch. It doesn't take long to finish the sear off, the last one I did took about 30 seconds of flame time total, but it depends on your tastes.

Step 5: Pour Pan Juices on Steak

If you have any juices in the pan, pour them over the steak since the torch's heat can dry out the crust a bit. The added juices will also help re-crisp the crust while it's still hot. Don't have any juices in the pan? You can reheat the juices from your sous vide bag in a separate pan during the sear and use that. And now it's time to eat.

BASIC RECIPES TO MASTER

NEW YORK STRIP

 5 mins    1h30 mins

New York Strips are one of the most iconic cuts of steak in the United States, and for great reason. This strip of meat is super tender and only gets even more tender from cooking it sous vide. It's recommended to cook highly marbled steaks, such as ribeyes and some strip steaks, at slightly higher temperatures. This is because fat renders better at higher temperatures - and you want rendered fat in steaks instead of chewy non--melted fat. I prefer cooking my sous vide New York strip steaks at 135F for 1-2 hours. This combination of time and temperature results in an incredibly tender NY strip with rendered fat.

TIP: Sear your New York strip a bit longer on the side with the fat cap. Rendering this fat adds amazing flavor to your steak!

INGREDIENTS

» New York Strip Steaks
» Sea Salt
» Cracked Black Pepper
» Avocado Oil (or another high smoke point oil)

RARE	MEDIUM RARE	MEDIUM	MEDIUM WELL	WELL DONE
122°F - 128°F	129°F - 135°F	136°F - 145°F	146°F - 155°F	156°F +
1 - 2 hours	1 - 2 hours	1 - 2 hours	1 - 2 hours	1 - 2 hours

DIRECTIONS

PREPARE IT

1. Pre-heat water bath to your ideal temperature (see chart on the side). We prefer 135°F, since the slightly higher temperature helps render some of the fat on the New York Strip.

2. Generously season with sea salt, cracked black pepper, and any aromatics such as rosemary.

3. Vacuum seal the NY Strip steak or place it in a heavy duty Ziploc bag using the water displacement method.

COOK IT

4. Place bagged NY Strip steak in water bath and cook for 1 - 2 hours (closer to 2 hours if steak is extra thick).

5. Remove New York strip steak and pat dry with paper towels.

SEAR IT

6. Pre-heat cast iron pan on medium-high heat and add avocado oil (or another high smoke point oil).

7. Sear steak on hot cast iron pan for approximately 1 minute, flipping every 15 seconds.

8. Add butter and any aromatics to the pan for added flavor and crispness. Sear for an additional 30 seconds. Make sure to also sear the strip of fat on the side!

9. (Optional) Break out the searing torch if you're feeling adventurous for a perfect crust.

SERVE IT

10. Before serving, use a spoon to top the New York Strip with the leftover juices and butter from the pan - this will help further develop the crust and add flavor.

11. Cut against the grain. Enjoy!

FILET MIGNON

 10 mins    1h30 mins

The most tender of cuts. Filet mignon is an exceptionally classy cut of steak with a butter-like, mouthwatering texture. Sous vide enhances this texture even more so, resulting in the most tender steak you can possibly eat. Since filet mignon does not have very much fat throughout, such as a ribeye, it's recommended to eat at rare to medium-rare temperatures.

INGREDIENTS

- » 2 Filet Mignon
- » Sea Salt
- » Cracked Black Pepper
- » Avocado Oil (or another high smoke point oil)

RARE	MEDIUM RARE	MEDIUM	MEDIUM WELL	WELL DONE
122°F - 128°F	129°F - 135°F	136°F - 145°F	146°F - 155°F	156°F +
1 - 2 hours	1 - 2 hours	1 - 2 hours	1 - 2 hours	1 - 2 hours

DIRECTIONS

PREPARE IT

1. (Optional) Marinate filet mignon for 24 hours prior.
2. Pre-heat water bath to your ideal temperature (see chart on the right). We prefer 130°F as filet mignon does not have much fat to tender.
3. Generously season with sea salt, cracked black pepper, and any aromatics such as rosemary.
4. Vacuum seal the filet mignon or place it in a heavy duty Ziploc bag using the water displacement method.

COOK IT

5. Place packaged filet mignon in water bath and cook for 1 - 2 hours (closer to 2 hours if steak is extra thick).
6. Remove filet mignon and pat dry with paper towels.

SEAR IT

7. Pre-heat cast iron pan on medium-high heat and add avocado oil (or another high smoke point oil).
8. Sear steak on hot cast iron pan for 1 minute, flipping every 15 seconds.
9. Add butter and any aromatics to the pan for added flavor and crispness. Sear for an additional 30 seconds to 1 minute.
10. (Optional) Break out the searing torch if you're feeling adventurous for a perfect crust.

SERVE IT

11. Before serving, top the filet mignons with the leftover juices from the pan.

FLANK STEAK

 5 mins    1h30 mins

Flank steaks are not just for stir-frying anymore! This traditionally tough and lean cut of meat turns into an amazingly tender cut of steak after cooking it sous vide. And best of yet? You can put together an incredible sous vide flank steak dish for next to nothing. Flank steaks are so cheap in your local grocery stores, making it a perfect cut of meat for cooking sous vide. Try out this sous vide flank steak recipe, you won't be disappointed!

TIP: Cut in thin strips against the grain for additional tenderness.

INGREDIENTS

- Flank Steak
- Sea Salt
- Cracked Black Pepper
- Avocado Oil (or another high smoke point oil)

RARE	MEDIUM RARE	MEDIUM	MEDIUM WELL	WELL DONE
122°F - 128°F 1 - 2 hours	129°F - 135°F 1 - 2 hours	136°F - 145°F 1 - 2 hours	146°F - 155°F 1 - 2 hours	156°F + 1 - 2 hours

DIRECTIONS

PREPARE IT

1. (Optional) Marinate flank steak for 24 hours prior. Flank steaks take marinade very well and it can even help make the meat more tender.

2. Pre-heat water bath to your ideal temperature (see chart on the side). We prefer 130°F since flank steaks do not have much fat to render.

3. Generously season with sea salt, cracked black pepper, and any aromatics such as rosemary.

4. Vacuum seal the flank steak or place it in a heavy duty Ziploc bag using the water displacement method.

COOK IT

5. Place bagged flank steak in water bath and cook for 1 - 2 hours (closer to 2 hours if steak is extra thick).

6. Remove flank steak and pat dry with paper towels.

SEAR IT

7. Pre-heat cast iron pan on medium-high heat and add avocado oil (or another high smoke point oil).

8. Sear steak on hot cast iron pan for approximately 1 minute, flipping every 15 seconds.

9. Add butter and any aromatics to the pan for added flavor and crispness. Sear for an additional 30 seconds.

10. (Optional) Break out the searing torch if you're feeling adventurous for a perfect crust.

SERVE IT

11. Before serving, use a spoon to top the flank steak with

TRI-TIP

⏱ 10 mins   ⏱ 7h

Tri-tip steaks are often an unheard of cut, especially if you live on the east coast. This traditionally tougher cut of steak has perhaps one of the most substantial transformations from sous vide. Coming in at a cost per pound that's usually half the cost of strip steaks, if not more, tri-tips are the ultimate sous vide steak. Perhaps the best part is that they are also usually 2lbs or more, which will likely leave a few leftovers for incredible cheesesteaks.

INGREDIENTS

- Tri-Tip Steak
- Sea Salt
- Cracked Black Pepper
- Avocado Oil (or another high smoke point oil)

RARE	MEDIUM RARE	MEDIUM	MEDIUM WELL	WELL DONE
122°F - 128°F	129°F - 135°F	136°F - 145°F	146°F - 155°F	156°F +
1 - 2 hours	1 - 2 hours	1 - 2 hours	1 - 2 hours	1 - 2 hours

DIRECTIONS

PREPARE IT

1. Pre-heat water bath to your ideal temperature (see chart on the side).

2. Generously season with sea salt, cracked black pepper, and any aromatics such as rosemary.

3. Vacuum seal the steak or place it in a heavy duty Ziploc bag using the water displacement method.

COOK IT

4. Place bagged steak in water bath and cook for roughly 7 hours.

5. Remove steak and pat dry with paper towels.

SEAR IT

6. Pre-heat cast iron pan on medium-high heat and add avocado oil (or another high smoke point oil).

7. Sear steak on hot cast iron pan for approximately 1 minute, flipping every 15 seconds.

8. Add butter and any aromatics to the pan for added flavor and crispness. Sear for an additional 30 seconds.

9. (Optional) Break out the searing torch if you're feeling adventurous for a perfect crust.

SERVE IT

10. Before serving, use a spoon to top the steak with the leftover juices and butter from the pan - this will help further develop the crust and add flavor.

11. Cut against the grain.

CORNED BEEF

 10 mins  7h

Corned beef resurfaces every year as a popular dish around St. Patrick's Day. This salt--cured beef is one of my favorites, whether it's corned beef and cabbage or making the world's best sandwich - A REUBEN! I make corned beef year-round for the sole purpose of making reuben sandwiches and sous vide makes it much easier. Traditional methods of making corned beef usually end up too flaky and does not slice well. With sous vide, you can control the temperature to the perfect level, allowing you to obtain the traditional taste and texture you know and love, while also enabling easy sandwich slicing. This sous vide corned beef recipe is perfect for corned beef and cabbage and then using the leftovers for reuben sandwiches!

INGREDIENTS

» Pre-Packaged (Store-Bought) Corned Beef

TRADITIONAL	LESS FLAKY, TENDER	SMOOTH
185°F	175°F	165°F
7 hours	8 hours	10 hours

DIRECTIONS

PREPARE IT

1. (Optional) If you're using a store-bought corned beef, I recommend submerging the corned beef in a large bowl of water and placing it in the fridge for 24 hours. When cooking store-bought corned beef sous vide, it can be too salty without rinsing some of it off.

2. Pre-heat water bath to your ideal temperature (see chart on the right). We prefer 185°F as it resembles traditional corned beef.

COOK IT

3. Vacuum seal your beef (without the spice packet added) and fully submerge in water bath. Cook based on the time chart on the side.

4. Remove corned beef and pat dry with paper towels.

5. (Optional) Add spice packet to the beef and let chill in the fridge for 24 hours, as it aids in slicing the beef.

SERVE IT

6. Use a sharp carving knife to slice thin layers of the corned beef.

7. If eating by itself or with cabbage, add slices to a freezer bag and re-heat in your water bath at 135F.

8. If eating on a sandwich, such as a Reuben, there's no need to reheat!

PORK TENDERLOIN

 10 mins    1h 30 mins

Pork tenderloin. Why don't we hear of this more often? This beautiful, tender cut of meat is often overlooked while perusing the meat section of your local grocery store. I think this is because most home cooks think pork has to be cooked to 160 degrees F for safety reasons - and 160F pork is DRY. But... did you know eating pink pork is about as safe as eating pink beef? Even MORE safe when factoring in the pasteurization time of sous vide.

Long story short, sous vide pork tenderloin is an unsung hero of the cheap-yet-delicious meals and is one of our favorite things to cook.

INGREDIENTS

» 1 Pork Tenderloin
» Marinade of Choice

MEDIUM RARE	MEDIUM	MEDIUM WELL	WELL DONE
130°F	140°F	150°F	160°F
1.5 hours	1.5 hours	1.5 hours	1.5 hours

DIRECTIONS

PREPARE IT

1. (Optional) Marinate pork tenderloin for 24 hours.

2. Pre-heat water bath to your ideal temperature (see chart on the right). We prefer 140°F.

3. Vacuum seal the pork tenderloin or place it in a heavy duty Ziploc bag using the water displacement method.

COOK IT

4. Place packaged pork tenderloin in water bath and cook for 1 - 3 hours.

5. Remove tenderloin and pat dry with paper towels.

SEAR IT

6. Pre-heat cast iron pan on medium-high heat and add avocado oil (or another high smoke point oil).

7. Sear on hot cast iron pan using for 1 minute, flipping every 15 seconds.

8. Add butter and any aromatics to the pan for added flavor and crispness. Sear for an additional 30 or so.

9. (Optional) Break out the searing torch if you're feeling adventurous for a perfect crust.

SERVE IT

10. Cut the pork tenderloin in half-inch to inch-sized slices. If desired, serve with pan sauce made from bag juices and remaining marinade.

PORK CHOP

 10 mins  1h 30 mins

Moving into a more common cut of the pig, pork chops are a staple of many Sunday dinners. Personally, I prefer bone-in pork chops, but this is completely up to your personal preference. Pork chops are one of the few cuts of meat that I nearly always marinate beforehand. Whether you're in the mood for something with a bit of kick, such as a mojo marinade, or something a bit sweeter, such as a honey glaze, your sous vide pork chop will be absolutely incredible!

INGREDIENTS

» Pork Chops (Bone-in or Boneless)
» Marinade of Choice

MEDIUM RARE	MEDIUM	MEDIUM WELL	WELL DONE
130°F 1.5 hours	140°F 1.5 hours	150°F 1.5 hours	160°F 1.5 hours

DIRECTIONS

PREPARE IT

1. (Optional) Marinate pork chops for 24 hours.

2. Pre-heat water bath to your ideal temperature (see chart on left). We prefer 140°F.

3. Vacuum seal the pork or place it in a heavy duty Ziploc bag using the water displacement method.

COOK IT

4. Place packaged pork chop in water bath and cook for 1 - 2 hours (add an hour if extra thick chop).

5. Remove pork and pat dry with paper towels.

SEAR IT

6. Pre-heat cast iron pan on medium--high heat and add avocado oil (or another high smoke point oil).

7. Sear on hot cast iron pan using for 1 minute, flipping every 15 seconds.

8. Add butter and any aromatics to the pan for added flavor and crispness. Sear for an additional 30 or so.

9. (Optional) Break out the searing torch if you're feeling adventurous for a perfect crust.

SERVE IT

10. If desired, serve with pan sauce made from bag juices and remaining marinade.

CHICKEN BREAST

 10 mins    1h 30 mins

Sous vide chicken breast is *unbelievably* easy to make. The first time you eat it, you will be shocked at just how juicy chicken can really be. Whether you like your chicken well done and stringy or tender and super juicy, using sous vide will absolutely produce the best results. Simply sear the chicken breast in a cast iron pan with a few aromatics and you have an incredibly easy way to make the best chicken you've ever had.

Tip: Trying to eat healthier? Meal prep! Cook up a week's worth of chicken on Sunday to have for lunch throughout the week - sous vide makes it so easy.

INGREDIENTS

- » Chicken breast
- » Sea Salt
- » Cracked Black Pepper
- » Avocado oil (or another high smoke point oil)
- » Rosemary Sprigs

JUICY	MEDIUM	WELL DONE
140°F	150°F	160°F

DIRECTIONS

PREPARE IT

1. Pre-heat water bath to your ideal temperature (see chart on the side). I prefer 150°F.

2. Generously season with sea salt and cracked black pepper.

3. Vacuum seal the chicken breasts with a few rosemary sprigs or place them in a heavy duty Ziploc bag using the water displacement method.

COOK IT

4. Place bagged chicken in water bath and cook for 1 - 3 hours, closer to 3 hours if your chicken is thick.

5. Remove chicken from the water and pat dry with paper towels very well.

SEAR IT

6. Pre-heat cast iron pan on medium-high heat and add avocado oil (or another high smoke point oil).

7. Sear chicken on hot cast iron pan until golden brown.

8. (Optional) Break out the searing torch if you're feeling adventurous for a perfect sear.

SERVE IT

9. Slice against the grain.

BONE-IN CHICKEN THIGHS

 10 mins    1h 15 mins

Let's face it, chicken thighs are nothing without a crispy, crunchy, salty, skin. Sous vide chicken thighs are incredibly moist and tender, however the outer layer of skin is lacking desire. That's why, when cooking sous vide chicken thighs, the most important part is searing. This recipe is for chili lime chicken thighs, which uses San Francisco Salt Co.'s amazing Chili Lime sea salt. You can change up the seasonings and marinades as you like; the rest of the cooking steps remain the same.

Tip: Find a long sleeve shirt and some oven mitts, because you'll need lots of oil in that hot pan!

INGREDIENTS

- 4 Bone-in Chicken Thighs
- SF Salt Co.'s Chili Lime Sea Salt
- Cracked Black Pepper
- Avocado oil (or another high smoke point oil)

- MARINADE (OPTIONAL)
- Store-bought mojo marinade
- 3 Chilis
- 2 Limes

JUICY	TRADITIONAL
155°F	165°F

74 SIMPLY SOUS VIDE

DIRECTIONS

PREPARE IT

1. Marinate chicken thighs for 24 hours prior by combining the chicken, Mojo sauce, slices chilis, and sliced limes, into a large bowl.

2. Pre-heat water bath to your ideal temperature (see chart on the side). I prefer 165°F, since I like these more traditional.

3. Generously season with SF Salt Co.'s Chili Lime sea salt and cracked black pepper.

4. Vacuum seal the chicken thighs or place them in a heavy duty Ziploc bag using the water displacement method.

COOK IT

5. Place bagged chicken thighs in water bath and cook for 1 - 2 hours.

6. Remove chicken thighs from the water and pat dry with paper towels very well. The surface must be very dry in order to obtain a good sear on the skin.

SEAR IT

7. Pre-heat cast iron pan on medium-high heat and add avocado oil (or another high smoke point oil).

8. Sear chicken thighs SKIN SIDE DOWN on hot cast iron pan until golden brown. If the chicken does not move easily when you go to flip, that means it's likely not ready to flip. Don't rip the skin off!

9. (Optional) Break out the searing torch if you're feeling adventurous for a perfect sear.

SERVE IT

10. Before serving, top the chicken thighs with more Chili Lime sea salt.

RACK OF LAMB

 10 mins    1 to 3 hours

It's official. Rack of lamb should not be cooked using any method other than sous vide. It's just too perfect. With just a little salt and pepper, sous vide rack of lamb has the most buttery, mouthwatering, and tender flavors imaginable. There's seriously no way to screw it up. Make it!

Tip: Use a torch after pan searing to help get a nice crust in the hard to reach places of the lamb rack.

INGREDIENTS

- 1 Rack of Lamb
- Sea Salt
- Cracked Black Pepper
- 1 Tbs Avocado Oil (or another high smoke point oil)
- 1 Tbs Butter

RARE	MEDIUM RARE	MEDIUM	MEDIUM WELL	WELL DONE
125°F	135°F	145°F	155°F	165°F

DIRECTIONS

PREPARE IT

1. (Optional) Marinate rack of ribs for 24 hours prior. We typically just use salt/pepper, but do enjoy a nice rosemary balsamic marinade with rack of lamb.

2. Pre-heat water bath to your ideal temperature (see chart on the right). We prefer 135°F which is on the high end of medium rare.

3. Generously season with sea salt, cracked black pepper, and any aromatics such as rosemary.

4. Vacuum seal your rack of ribs.

COOK IT

5. Place bagged rack of lamb in water bath and cook for 1 - 3 hours.

6. Remove lamb rack and pat dry with paper towels.

SEAR IT

7. Pre-heat cast iron pan on medium-high heat and add avocado oil (or another high smoke point oil).

8. Sear lamb rack on hot cast iron pan for 1 minute, rotating every 15 seconds or so. Be sure to rotate the lamb in order to get as much surface contact as possible.

9. Add butter and any aromatics to the pan for added flavor and crispness. Sear for an additional 30 seconds to 1 minute.

10. (Optional) Use a torch to get in the nooks and crannies of the rack of lamb.

SERVE IT

11. Slice your rack of lamb after every 2 ribs with a sharp knife.

SEAFOOD

SALMON WITH HOLLANDAISE SAUCE

 20 mins    1 hr 15 mins

This simple sous vide salmon recipe transforms a regular salmon filet into an elegant dish thanks to hollandaise sauce. Did I use simple and hollandaise in the same sentence? Hollandaise is notoriously tricky; not because of the ingredients or individual steps to make it, but because of timing. If you've ever made eggs benedict you'll know that timing the hollandaise sauce with seared Canadian bacon, toasted English muffins, and perfectly poached eggs can be a bit challenging. Thanks to sous vide, we can make the easiest hollandaise sauce ever. How easy? You literally toss all of the ingredients into a bag and cook it - don't even mix it beforehand.

The best part about this two-for-one recipe is that once you combine all of the ingredients for the hollandaise sauce and cook it for 45 minutes, you can actually leave the sauce in the water bath while you finish cooking the salmon for another 30 minutes. No more worrying about timing and having a cold sauce. Once the salmon is ready to be pulled from your water bath, just toss the hollandaise mixture into a blender and serve.

INGREDIENTS

- » 2 fresh salmon filets
- » Salt for brining

DIRECTIONS

1. Dry brine salmon by generously salting both sides and place back in refrigerator for a minimum of 30 minutes.

2. Pre-heat water to 148F

3. Add all of ingredients for Hollandaise sauce into a large Ziploc bag. Mixing isn't important, since it will be blended later.

4. Submerge using the water displacement method and cook for 45 minutes.

5. Decrease your sous vide machine temperature to your desired salmon doneness (Rare - 110F; Medium Well - 140F). Note: Add ice or a few cups of cold water to speed this up.

6. Cook salmon for 30 - 45 minutes. I recommend using a ziploc bag here again, since salmon is a bit too fragile for many vacuum sealers.

7. Remove your Hollandaise mixture from the water bath and pour it into your blender. Blend on a medium speed until the mixture is a smooth light yellow. Note: your mixture will be very separated when removing from your sous vide bath - this is very normal.

8. Remove salmon, pat dry, and sear (if desired).

9. Serve with hollandaise sauce.

LOBSTER

 10 mins    1 hr

I'll be real with you here. The hardest part about cooking lobster now is being able to remove the meat from the tail. Sous vide lobster is crazy simple - one of the few proteins that do not need a sear after cooking. Literally drop the lobster tails and some butter in a bag, cook for an hour, and serve. It's 100% better than broiling, boiling, and steaming.

INGREDIENTS

- 2 Lobster Tails
- 10 Tbs Butter
- Fresh Parsley

SOFT TRANSLUCENT	TENDER	FIRM
120°F	130°F	140°F

DIRECTIONS

PREPARE IT

1. Preheat water bath to your desired temperature, based on the chart to the left.
2. Submerge frozen lobster tails in bowl of cold water for approximately 30 minutes to defrost and loosen up.

COOK IT

1. Place lobster tails, fresh parsley, and 2-3 Tbs of butter into a heavy duty Ziploc bag. Vacuum sealing is possible, however we prefer using the water displacement method as it is less likely to deform the shape of the tail.
2. Cook for 1 hour.

SERVE IT

1. Melt 6-8 Tbs of butter in a saucepan over medium heat. If you prefer clarified butter, heat until boiling and the butter fat separates.
2. Serve clarified butter on plate beneath tail, or in a separate bowl.
3. Cut shell down the middle with kitchen shears and slowly but firmly pull shell apart, ensuring not to rip the meat.
4. Gently remove lobster meat from shell and de-vein, if necessary.

EGGS

SOFT BOILED, POACHED, HARD BOILED

 0 mins    15 mins to 1 hr

Overcooked eggs are a thing of the past! With sous vide, it's so easy to get perfect eggs every single time. Whether you like soft egg whites, fully poached eggs, or easy hard boiled eggs, simply set the temperature according to your preferred type and drop them in - no need to bag them! Crack a poached egg over toast with avocado in the morning for an unbelievable start to your day.

INGREDIENTS
» Eggs

SOFT BOILED	POACHED	HARD BOILED
145°F 45 minutes	165°F 15 minutes	175°F 1 hour

DIRECTIONS

1. Preheat water bath to your desired temperature, using the provided chart to the left.
2. Cook the eggs for the prescribed time, then promptly remove and place in an ice bath for one minute.
3. Eat immediately or store for later.

EGG BITES

 15 mins    1 hr

Sous vide egg bites quickly became one of the most popular and frequently talked about recipes in the industry after Starbucks popularized them. These pillowy eggs have a fluffy texture yet creamy consistency due to the addition of cottage cheese. You will need small canning jars in order to use this recipe. Get creative by using your favorite breakfast ingredients to spice up your morning meals!

TIP: Place your additional ingredients, such as cooked bacon and sausage, into the bottom of the jars before pouring the egg mixture in. This will disperse them throughout the mixture instead of having all of the meat on top.

INGREDIENTS

- 8 Eggs
- ½ Cup Shredded Cheddar Cheese
- ½ cup cottage cheese
- ¼ Tsp Salt
- ¼ Tsp Pepper
- Other Breakfast Ingredients to Taste (Cooked Bacon/Sausage, Tomato, Mushrooms, Green Onions, etc)

DIRECTIONS

1. Preheat water bath to 172F.
2. Blend eggs, cheddar cheese, cottage cheese, salt, and pepper until smooth. Milky foam will rise to the top.
3. (Optional) Place any additional ingredients at the bottom of each jar, such as cooked bacon and sausage.
4. Pour egg mixture into each jar, dividing evenly.
5. Tighten canning jar lids using ONLY your fingertips, ensuring not to fully tighten as air must escape during the cooking process.
6. Cook for 1 hour.
7. Carefully remove from water bath using tongs and serve immediately or let chill on the counter until cool to touch (about 1 hour) followed by adding them to the refrigerator.
8. Looking to reheat? Simply microwave the egg bites (without lids) for 30 seconds.

EGGS BENEDICT

 25 mins    1 hr

Let's face it, making hollandaise sauce is difficult. Ok, maybe not by itself, but timing it in parallel with poached eggs and toasted muffins and seared bacon is a lot to manage. Thankfully to sous vide, making eggs benedict just got a whole lot easier. This sous vide eggs benedict recipe uses the same temperature to poach the eggs AND make the hollandaise sauce. It really can't get any easier.

INGREDIENTS

- » 2 English Muffins
- » 4 Eggs
- » 4 Slices Canadian Bacon
- » Butter
- » Fresh Chopped Parsley

HOLLANDAISE

- » 4 Tbs Butter
- » 1 Egg Yolk
- » 1 Tsp Lemmon Juice
- » 1 Tsp Water
- » 1/2 Shallot, diced
- » Pinch of Cayenne
- » Salt to taste

DIRECTIONS

PREPARE IT

1. Preheat Water to 148F
2. Add all of ingredients for Hollandaise sauce into a large Ziploc bag. Don't worry about mixing.
3. Place bag into water bath using the water displacement method.
4. Add the 4 eggs into the water bath. These can go straight into the water, or placed inside of another bag for easier removal when ready.

COOK IT

5. Cook for 1 hour
6. Sear your Canadian Bacon over medium high heat until done.
7. Halve your two English Muffins and toast them.
8. If necessary, place toasted English Muffins and Canadian Bacon into a preheated 250F oven to remain warm while you finish the sauce.

BLEND IT

9. Remove your Hollandaise mixture from the water bath and pour it into your blender. Blend on a medium speed until the mixture is a smooth light yellow. Note: your mixture will be very separated when removing from your sous vide bath - this is very normal.

CRACK IT

10. Using a split spoon, crack your poached eggs and discard excess/loose egg whites into a bowl.

SERVE IT

11. Place a poached egg onto each muffin/bacon.
12. Generously top with hollandaise sauce.
13. Top with finely chopped parsley, to taste.

VEGETABLES

ASPARAGUS

 10 mins    15 mins

Asparagus tastes great when it's seasoned well, but achieving a good consistency can be extremely difficult when cooking using traditional methods. If you're like me, your asparagus usually ends up chewy and hard to cut up. No longer with sous vide!

For only a short time at a high temperature, you can get asparagus that is perfectly cooked and a pleasure to eat. You can season the asparagus however you'd like, just butter works fine as does flavored olive oils.

INGREDIENTS

- 12 oz Trimmed Asparagus
- 1-2 Tbsp Olive oil (flavored or regular) or 2-3 Tbsp Butter
- 1 Tsp Garlic Powder
- Salt & Pepper as desired

DIRECTIONS

1. Preheat water bath to 185F/85C.
2. Wash asparagus and trim the tough end.
3. Combine all ingredients into your sous vide bag and seal.
4. Cook for 15 minutes.
5. (Optional) Remove the asparagus from the bag and sear using a pan or grill for 1-2 minutes for a crisp exterior.
6. Serve immediately.

HONEY GLAZED CARROTS

 10 mins    45-60 mins

Cooking carrots sous vide captures all of the intense carrot flavor within the bag while also retaining much more of the nutritional value. At 185F for just under an hour, you will experience the best carrots you've ever had – no more mushy veggies! Add a little bit of honey and cinnamon for a delicious glaze that even the kids will love.

INGREDIENTS

- 6-8 Medium to Large Sized Carrots, Washed and Peeled
- 3 Tbs Unsalted Butter
- 2 Tbs Honey
- 1 Cinnamon Stick
- Sea Salt to Taste

DIRECTIONS

1. Preheat water bath to 185F
2. Wash and peel carrots
3. Combine all ingredients into your sous vide bag and seal.
4. Cook for 45 minutes to 1 hour.
5. (Optional) Remove the carrots from the bag and sear on a hot pan or grill for 1-2 minutes to help caramelize the carrots.
6. Serve with sea salt and drizzled honey to taste.

DESSERTS

CRÈME BRULEE

 25 mins    1 hr

I've always enjoyed Crème Brûlée, with its glassy sugar top coating and silky smooth custard underneath. But this lemon raspberry sous vide Crème Brûlée recipe takes it to another level. This sous vide dessert recipe is perfect for entertaining and parties since you can make a bunch of 4oz servings very easily.

INGREDIENTS

- » 4 Cups Heavy Whipping Cream
- » 8 Egg Yolks
- » 1/2 Cup Sugar
- » 2 Tsp Vanilla Extract
- » ~2 Tbs Lemon Zest, depending how "lemony" you want it
- » 10-12 4oz Canning Jars

DIRECTIONS

PREPARE IT

1. Pre-heat water to 190F
2. Whisk the egg yolks and sugar together in a LARGE bowl. Set aside.
3. Add heavy whipping cream and vanilla extract to large sauce pan and cook on medium high heat until simmering. Continue simmering for 3 minutes then remove from heat.
4. Add lemon zest to sauce pan, mix well.
5. Slowly pour the cream into the egg mixture while whisking.

COOK IT

6. Divide cream mixture evenly across 4oz canning jars, leaving about 1/2" from the top of the jar.

7. Tighten canning jar lids using ONLY your fingertips, ensuring not to fully tighten as air must escape during the cooking process.

8. Carefully place jars into pre-heated water bath using tongs (Remember, 190F is hot. Really hot.)

9. Cook for 1 hour.

10. Remove and let sit on counter for an hour or until cool to the touch. Once cool, refrigerate at least 5 hours.

TORCH IT

11. Remove jar lids and lightly pat tops dry with paper towel if there is any excess water.

12. Sprinkle a thin coating of sugar on top.

13. Break out the kitchen torch and quickly melt the sugar (note: don't aim for the "burnt" look yet, we want the first layer just melted).

14. Add another light coating of sugar.

15. Use torch again to melt and caramelize the sugar to your desired amount. Be sure not to over-torch it, as the glass canning jars can shatter.

16. Top with fresh raspberries.

CHEESE CAKE

 20-30 mins    1 hr 30 mins

Similarly to the Crème Brûlée, these mini cheesecakes are also made in 4oz canning jars. Kids absolutely love them! I use a simple graham cracker crust at the base of the jar - if you have the time, pre-baking the crust in the jars for 10 minutes helps develop a traditional cheesecake crust. However, simply adding the crust mixture without baking still results in an amazing and fun dessert. When finished, top the dessert with your favorite fruit!

INGREDIENTS

- 16 oz Cream Cheese
- 3 Eggs
- ¾ Cup Sugar
- ½ Tbs Vanilla Extract
- ¼ Cup Sour Cream
- Fruit to top, if desired

CRUST

- ½ Package of Graham Crackers (About 4-5), Crushed
- 1 Tbs Sugar
- 3 Tbs Unsalted Butter, Melted
- ¼ Tsp Cinnamon

DIRECTIONS

1. Preheat water bath to 176F.
2. Crush graham crackers into very fine pieces. I place them in a sandwich bag and use a rolling pin.
3. Add sugar, melted butter, and cinnamon. Mix thoroughly.
4. Place crust mixture at the bottom of 8 4oz canning jars and firmly pack down.
5. (Optional) Bake crust and jars for 10 minutes at 350F.
6. Add room temperature cream cheese, eggs, sugar, sour cream, and vanilla into a large mixing bowl and mix thoroughly.
7. Add cheesecake mixture to each canning jar, leaving about ½ inch from the top.
8. Tighten canning jar lids using ONLY your fingertips, ensuring not to fully tighten as air must escape during the cooking process.
9. Cook for 1 hour 30 minutes.
10. Carefully remove from water bath using tongs and let chill on the counter until cool to touch (about 1 hour).
11. Place cheesecakes in refrigerator for at least 4 hours.
12. Open lid, top with fresh fruit or blueberry filling, and enjoy!

BANANAS FOSTER

 15 mins    25 mins

Bananas foster is an all-time great dessert! For authentic bananas foster, you will first need to make a rum sauce (be sure to bring it to a boil as described in order to remove most the alcohol). However, you can also eliminate the rum completely for an easy rum-less spiced bananas! Simply remove the rum and reduce the butter from 4 Tbsp to 2 Tbsp. Add all of the other ingredients in the bag and cook for 25 minutes.

INGREDIENTS

RUM SAUCE

- 2 Tbsp Dark Rum
- 4 Tbsp Butter
- 1 Tsp Vanilla
- 1/2 Cup Brown Sugar

SOUS VIDE INGREDIENTS

- 2 Bananas
- 1 Tsp Cinnamon
- (Optional) 1/4 Cup Chopped Pecans

DIRECTIONS: BANANAS FOSTER

1. Preheat water bath to 145F.
2. Combine all the rum sauce ingredients into a sauce pan, boil for 2 minutes.
3. Remove the sauce from heat and allow to start cooling down.
4. Peel and cut up your bananas, then add cinnamon.
5. Add bananas into your sous vide bag, then add ~3 Tbsp of your rum sauce and seal. Put the rest of the rum sauce into a container for later.
6. Cook the bananas for 25 minutes.
7. Remove the bananas from the bag and serve with vanilla ice cream when desired. You can cool or freeze the bananas, or eat them immediately.
8. (Optional) Drip more rum sauce over your dessert or sear the bananas quickly with a kitchen torch for that "something extra".

DIRECTIONS: RUM-LESS SPICED BANANAS

1. Preheat water bath to 145F.
2. Peel and cut your bananas.
3. Combine all ingredients into a ziplock bag and submerge into water bath using the water displacement method. Note: Remember to reduce the butter from 4 Tbps to 2 Tbps for the rum-less version.
4. Cook the bananas for 25 minutes.
5. Remove the bananas from the bag and serve with vanilla ice cream when desired. You can cool or freeze the bananas, or eat them immediately.
6. (Optional) Drip more sauce over your dessert or sear the bananas quickly with a kitchen torch for that "something extra".

WINE POACHED PEAR

 10 mins    50 mins

Red wine poached pears are elegantly delicious while also appearing as a work of art on your plate. And of course, sous vide makes poached pears a breeze. Simply combine all of the ingredients into a bag and cook for 45 minutes. Serve immediately from the bag with vanilla ice cream and you have a light, yet satisfying, romantic dessert for two.

INGREDIENTS

- 2 Pears, Firm
- 2 Cups Dry Red Wine
- 1 Cup Sugar
- 1 Cinnamon Stick
- 3 Cloves
- ~4 Slices of Orange Peel (Roughly 2 - 3 Inches)
- 1 Tsp Vanilla Extract

DIRECTIONS

1. Preheat water bath to 178F.
2. Carefully peel pears.
3. Combine ingredients into a large Ziploc bag and use the water displacement method to submerge in your water bath.
4. Cook for 45 minutes.
5. (Optional) Drink a glass of wine; I mean, you have it uncorked...
6. Carefully remove pears and either serve right from the bag or serve chilled, depending on preferences.
7. (Optional) Add the wine mixture to a saucepan and simmer on medium for roughly 15 - 20 minutes, or until the liquid thickens.
8. Serve with the wine syrup and vanilla ice cream.

Made in the USA
Middletown, DE
02 March 2018